CHORUS.
They shall be bow-men,
Freemen and yeomen,
Who, 'tis confess'd,
Did shoot the best
Before the butts to-day!

BUTCHER
Stand forth, Long Tom! Come forth, Big Ben!
Come forth, stand forth, ye proper men!

ALL.
Long Tom! Big Ben!

Enter LONG TOM *and* BIG BEN.

DUET.

(LONG TOM *and* BIG BEN.)

TOM.
We are two proper men,
Myself and Brother Ben;
We both are Royal keepers in the Forest!

BEN.
We're ever hand in glove—
Thou lovest what I love,
And I do ever hate what thou abhorrest!

TOM.
We're very like each other,
Are myself and younger brother,
And consequently people who have seen us—

BEN
Have mentioned that it odd is
How in our minds and bodies
There's such a little difference between us

BOTH.
But there *is* a little difference between us—
We're as like as pot and kettle,
Being made of self-same metal—
But there *is* a certain difference between us!

BEN.
And in the days to be,
The simple historee
Of Brother Tom and me may point a moral!

TOM.
That Cupid, when he comes
Between the best of chums,
Doth generally lead them to a quarrel!

BEN.
We both do love a maiden,
Our hearts with love are laden,
For each doth think his lady-love a Venus!

TOM
And I do say that *mine* is
As good a maid as *thine* is,
And that's the little difference between us!

BOTH.   Yes, *that's* the only difference between us!
　　　　And being men of mettle,
　　　　Our difference we'll settle,
　　　　Then there *won't* be any difference between us!

(*They begin to fight with quarter-staves.*)

MAY Q. (*coming down to them.*) ~~What now!~~ How now! If I am Queen of ~~Love~~ to-day I'll have no quarrellers in my court! ~~Have done, have done, I say~~! What's the pother? Do you both love the same maid?

BEN.   I love *thee*, while—

TAILOR.   Look you, a Tailor is as big a man as a Forester in his own way.

BUTCHER.   Out of *my* way! A Butcher is a better man than a Tailor.

BAKER.   And a Baker, too, may talk as loud as a Butcher, on occasion.

TINKER.   To say nought of a Tinker; and *I* say, "I love thee "—

OTHERS.   And I! And I! And I!

MAY Q.   Peace! Cupid hath taught ~~you to shoot your words straight.~~ I will shoot as straight as you—I love you not! (*To* TOM.) Will *you* shoot a round with me? What say *you*!

TOM.   I say you are indeed a fair maid, yet I love you not.

MAY Q. ~~That arrow wobbles. It is too long for the bow. Trim it of " You are a fair maid," and let fly.~~ " I love you not "; 'tis enough to wound a woman with!

TOM.   I would not wound thee, nor any woman.

MAY Q.   Oddsfish! Have no fear of wounding *me*, my man! I am heart-whole for all your "I love you not"!

BEN.   He is bewitched!

MAY Q.   How?

BEN.   Why, by witchcraft!

MAY Q.   Whose?

BEN.   Why, a witch's! And they say, by the same token, that when you talk of the devil—who is the father of witches—

Enter JILL. (*She carries a cat in her arms.*)

MAY Q.   What's brought you here?

JILL.   My two legs.

MAY Q. Witch!

JILL. This and that!

MAY Q. I say you are a witch!

JILL. Some say what they do not know, and some know what they cannot say. But I will say what I know—listen!

[handwritten: lay down for this though —>]
I know that love
  Is far above
All jewels that are seen,
And I do know
  That being so
'Tis wanted by a queen!
But love I ween
  May pass her by,
So I may laugh,
  While she may sigh—
  I wonder why?

[handwritten: Return to throne and sit while Jill sings her song.]

BUTCHER. Who do you dream would love *you*, you drab?

JILL. Why, first, my cat here, and second, a better man than you, or the dream would be a nightmare! And third (to MAY QUEEN) marry, a better man than *you*—if love leads to marriage. But if not a cat or a man—why, the birds and the deer and such wild forest things. For I am one of them! I am one of them!

SONG.

JILL.

Oh, where the deer do lie
  There dwell I!
Far in the forest shade,
Down in the dappled glade—
  Oh, what a life!
    Throw her a bone!
  Nobody's wife—
    Jill-all-alone!

Where Herne the Hunter rides
  Jill abides;
I hear the ghostly sounds,
Herne's phantom horn and hounds—
  Oh, she's a witch!
    Pick up a stone!
  Die in a ditch—
    Jill-all-alone!

> But when the morning breaks
>   And awakes
> All other forest things,
> Jill too awakes and sings—
>   Oh, the sweet day!
>   Queen on a throne!
>   Merry as May—
>   Jill-all-alone!

MAY Q. Now, what game shall we choose to suit May Day?

JILL. What shall you play? Why, the game of real life—a real Queen with a real Court. Can anything be merrier? My cat shall tell you how Queen Bess fares. (*To cat.*) What do you say? Of a truth—of a truth! My Lord of Essex stands on one side of the throne—so. (*To BEN.*) Do you stand for the Earl of Essex. And Sir Walter Raleigh on the other side—so; the side of the Queen's heart. (*To TOM, on left of MAY QUEEN.*) And Mistress Throckmorton, the maid of honour, is somewhere— wherever Sir Walter's thoughts are, though the Queen knows it not. And so they play "he loves me, he loves me not."

Enter WILKINS *with* SIMKINS.

WIL. And what would you have *me* play?

JILL. You? Do you play the fool, who laughs at love like a wise man; because it is wiser to laugh at a thing than to weep with it.   [*Exit.*

WIL. True! Very true!

SIM. But, the fool! You play the fool! Know you *him!* The leading player in Shakespeare's company—to whom I play second, humbly—nay, proudly! (*Aside.*) Flatter him so, and he'll wag his ass's ears to any tune you pipe! (*Aloud.*) Prince of players! King of comedians! A fool indeed! (*Aside.*) A fool in very deed!

WIL. Hush, friend—you are fulsome.   I am indeed Master Walter Wilkins, Poet and Chief Player in Will Shakespeare's company; and for his profit I prophesy that he hath a misconception of the part of a writer in writing a part, in that he hath too little regard for the matters of singing and dancing; for a time will come when all comedies shall be musical, or the public will have none of them—not even if I played the chief part, and so made the part seem greater than the whole. It is so I have counselled Will Shakespeare as I do you: song and dance, my masters, song and dance—or let the drama die a dull dog that is hanged on its own tag!

SONG.

WILKINS.

I do counsel that your playtime be a jocund and a gay time,
    And your player be as merry as he can;
If a play be glum and gloomy—very tragical and " tomby "—
    I do act upon a very proper plan:
As a patriotic Briton I have pondered on and written
    A jolly sailor song, about the sea,
With a hornpipe (though perchance one be incongruous) I dance
      one,
      Whatever kind of character I be.
        And the time will come—
        'Twill be seen by some
          (Though not perchance by me)—
        When a dance will act like magic,
        While *five* acts that are tragic—
          Well, that's where I and Shakespeare disagree

There's no character but—marry! 'tis convenient to carry
    At any time the burden of a song!
One word will introduce it, and the public will excuse it,
    And, oddsbodikins! applaud it, loud and long!
Now in Hamlet's long soliloquy he mentioneth the billow—
    Dost remember in " To be, or not to be "?
Come the words " a sea of trouble "—the applause, I trow, would
      double
      If he forthwith sang a song *about* the sea!
        And the time will come—
        'Twill be seen by some
          (Though not perchance by me)—
        When a lively Prince of Denmark
        Will sing that song, and *then* mark
          How entirely I and Shakespeare disagree!
          (*Dance.*)   [*Exit.*

TOM. Were I indeed Sir Walter Raleigh, and the Queen loving me and I not loving the Queen, because of my love for a maid of honour, I would, if I were a man of honour and Sir Walter Raleigh—

Enter RALEIGH.

RAL. Well, friend; if you were I—what then?

TOM. Nay, sir; I was speaking my thoughts aloud.

RAL. 'Tis a dangerous malady in these times. If it grow upon you, let a leech look at your tongue—to cut it off. It may save your head.

BEN. Sir, do not be angry with my brother. He hath been fearfully bewitched by a wild wench who dwells in the forest. He claims her to be as sweet a maid as our May Queen. I did set about cudgelling my brains to find a cure for him, till he set about cudgelling mine.

MAY Q. There are but two cures for witchcraft—to burn the witch or drown her in a sack.

RAL. If she be a witch. They nearly burned me for a wizard when I first burned tobacco! But who'll think of witches on May Day? Better drown such thoughts—and here comes the sack to drown them in.

Enter a Vendor of wine and mead.

VENDOR. Who'll buy my mead or sack?
    Four gills to the pint, and a quart to a Black Jack!
    Who'll drink my mead or sack?

RAL. Why, every Jack of us here—at my expense. And see that every Jack has his complement of Jills, as the song goes. (*Taking a Black Jack.*) Marry, 'tis a very Falstaff of wine-cups!

SONG AND CHORUS.

RALEIGH.

That every Jack should have a Jill
    Dame Nature always meant, sirs;
But where's the gill can hope to fill
    This Jack to his content, sirs?
Since three or four of gills or more
    Do make his proper measure,
Give Jack his mead, and Jack indeed
    Will bubble high with pleasure!

        Then here's a lack
          Of care that kills,
        When every Jack
          Hath all his gills
          Of what he wills,
        Or mead or sack,
          For they're the Jills
        For fat Black Jack!

Now, Jack will lay you on the ground
    If you stay long together,
For I'll be bound, though fat and round,
    He is as tough as leather!
And who so wills to steal his Jills
    Will find it is a tussle,
Till on his back he's laid by Jack,
    For Jack's a man of muscle!

        But here's a lack &c.   [*Exit.*

MAY Q. Now listen to me! A witch is a witch, whether it be May Day or Christmas. *and what's fairer game for*

BUTCHER. ~~The same with a butcher—'tis a steady trade and a sticking trade.~~

TINKER. ~~The same with a—~~

MAY Q. ~~Let such as wish my favour favour my wishes. A witch is fair game and ever in season.~~ And what's a fairer game for a May Day than a witch hunt? Who says a witch hunt?

CROWD. I! And I! And I!

BUT. A hue and cry! A witch! A witch!

BEN. Hue! Hue! A witch hunt!

ALL. Hue! Hue! Hue! A witch! A witch! Hue! Hue!

[*Exeunt all, except* MAY QUEEN, KATE, *and* TOM.

TOM. They'll not catch her, for she runs like a deer. But if they do—and do her harm—well, I will not kill thee, even then, for my brother's sake.

MAY Q. Your brother's sake! What is your brother to me—or what are you? *cross left*

TOM. I have thought that you liked me, a little, and I would have liked you—

MAY Q. Yes? *delighted*

TOM. To like my brother.

MAY Q. ~~Must it be always you, or your brother? Now listen.~~ I hate big men. It is brain that women worship—brain, fool, not bulk; as is shown by the way I am attracted to—to Master Wilkins.

Enter WILKINS.

WIL. Who speaks my name?

MAY Q. Did I speak it—aloud? I was thinking. It hath a sweet sound—" Walter Wilkins." Yes, it is a pretty name.

WIL. And famous.

Enter RALEIGH.

MAY Q. What think you, Master Wilkins, of love at first sight?

WIL. Why, love seems a merry thing at first sight—and I have never looked further.

RAL. Then sigh not for second sight—or you may prophesy differently.

WIL. I prophesy indifferently, sir; but if love come to me, 'twill find me merry, or not at all.

RAL. To laugh at love is fool's wisdom.

WIL. To weep with it is wise man's folly, sir.

RAL. Perhaps. I like your humour.

WIL. My humour is good humour, sir—that is my rule of life, and I apply it to love. *I come down to wilkins right*

QUINTET.

MAY QUEEN, KATE, RALEIGH, WILKINS, *and* TOM.

Love is meant to make us glad,
　Hey, jolly, jolly little Cupid!
Fools do let him make them sad,
　Hey, folly, folly, they are stupid!
　　　Let's be wise
　　　　If we do meet him,
　　　Heave no sighs
　　　　But gladly greet him!
And say to him " Good day " to him,
　He'll treat us as we treat him!
Hey, jolly, jolly little Love!
　Sorrow follows folly,
　As the berries grow on holly,
　And oh, 'tis folly
　　　To be afraid of Love!
Love is but a butterfly,
　Hey, jolly! What is there to match it?
Will you watch it flutter by?
　Oh, folly, folly not to catch it!
　　　Try to keep
　　　　It when you've caught it!
　　　Wherefore weep
　　　　If you have sought it?
To sigh for it, and die for it.
　Oh, wisdom never taught it!
Hey, jolly, jolly little Love!
　Sorrow follows folly,
　As the berries grow on holly,
　And oh, 'tis folly
　　　To run away from Love!

　　　　　　　us and sit left
　　　　　　　[*Exeunt* TOM *and* KATE.

WIL. Ah, sir, 'tis in his treatment of lovers that I would read Shakespeare a lesson; that it is pleasanter to make love go with laughter than with tears.

RAL. He has studied life.

WIL. No, sir—death. To live is not the fashion with his lovers; they would sooner die than marry, so it seems. And to turn events the other way were as easy as the alphabet. Think of his Romeo and Juliet, and what it might have been had I written it! Now mark—

A. was the Angel he met at the ball;
B. was her beauty apparent to all;
C. is for Capulet (name which she bore);
D. the disguise which young Romeo wore;
E. for the Ease of his elegant pose;
F. the Fandango they danced on their toes;
G. the Guitar which he played by and bye,
H. for her Handkerchief dropped in reply;
(I am young Romeo, breathing his love;
J. is for Juliet sitting above!)
K. the last Kiss as apart they are torn
L. by the Lark who's the " herald of morn "
M. is the Moon that's preparing to set;
N. is the Nurse calling, " Come, Juliet! "
O is the ejaculation she sighed,
P. because promised as Paris's bride;
Q. are the Quarrels that quickly ensued;
R. are the Rapiers drawn in the feud;
S. for the Sentence pronounced by the " Dook "
T. for the Tragical Turn events took;
U. is the Unhappy end of the play;
V. is the Version which *I'*ll write some day:
W. Shakespeare's an Xcellent writer,
But Wise Editors will say *my* version's brighter!

[*Exit with* MAY QUEEN.

Enter BESSIE. (*She is gathering flowers, and sings.*)

SONG.

BESSIE.

She had a letter from her love,
    And on her heart she laid it:
'Twas all in rhyme, and Father Time
    She vowed could never fade it!
        Ah me! a lover's vow—
        She knoweth better now!

She lost the letter from her love,
    Or somebody did steal it;
And oh, the smart of her poor heart,
    She vowed that naught could heal it!
        Ah me! a lover's vow—
        She knoweth better now!

She found the letter from her love,
    When she had sorely missed it;
And spite the stain of mud and rain,
    She fondled it and kissed it!
        Ah me! a lover's vow—
        She knoweth better now!

RAL. Bessie, what do the words of that song mean?

BESS. What do the words of a song matter, if the tune be right? What matter if a girl's heart break, if her face smile?

RAL. Are you going?

BESS. Yes. By your leave, I will take mine.

RAL. Whither?

BESS. Away—to change my gown, to attend the Queen.

RAL. I love you in a simple dress. (*Coming to her.*) Do you know what love is?

BESS. I was taught once.

RAL. When?

BESS. Why, when I learned my Latin grammar—thus: Love, which is masculine, should be declined in all cases.

RAL. When its cases are plural. In my case, it is alone— the one love of my life.

BESS. Then it is singular.

RAL. Love may be a verb, conjugated thus: I love, thou lovest, and that's enough; for it requires no third person present.

BESS. Ah! For the present. But how of other moods and other tenses, the future and the past?

RAL. I vow—

BESS. I trow your vows are good vows as lovers' vows go. They have served for the Queen before me, so I should not complain.

RAL. You speak bitterly.

BESS. But I smile sweetly?

RAL. In very truth.

BESS. And in very truth the words of my song were true, and mean much to both of us. " She lost the letter from her love." And so have I! Oh, if your letter be found and brought to the Queen!

RAL. What then?

BESS. Why, then, the air of Court would be bad for both of us!

RAL. Let's have done with it now, you and I! What is it they sing in the Tales of Robin Hood, in their Morris Dance to-day?

" Then who would not be out of Court
        As Robin Hood befell,
    To fare as Love may bid him fare
        And bid all else farewell?
    If Love follow him
        Beneath the greenwood tree."

Aye! It is when a man's in love that the quiet of country calls him loudest. Is it so with a maid? Would you give up your life in Court for me?

BESS. In Court, or elsewhere, I would give up my life for thee!

DUET.

RALEIGH and BESSIE.

RAL. When true love hath found a man,
He will hear the pipe of Pan;
  Pan, the god of open country,
  Oh, his tunes are pretty!
Nature bids you bring your sweet one
Where no other soul may meet one;
  " Nature made the country side,
    And man did make the city."*

        Come, come to Arcadie!
        Bring your Phyllis, happy Corydon!
        Learn together, if you can,
        The simple tunes of Piper Pan!

BESS. When a maid doth love a man,
She will hear the pipe of Pan;
  Pan will call her, call her, call her,
    With a magic ditty!
Better far a country cottage
If your true love share your pottage,
  Than to dwell in Castle Pride,
    As some do—more's the pity!

        Come, come to Arcadie!
        I'll be Phyllis, you be Corydon!
        Happy maid and happy man,
        To dance all day for Piper Pan!

                    [Dance. Exeunt.

Enter ESSEX, with a Lord.

ESSEX. There goes a lesson in love—and the madness of
lovers! For there goes one who prefers the good looks of Bessie
Throckmorton to the good books of Bessie of England!

LORD. 'Twould ruin Raleigh—if the news could be brought to
the Queen's ears!

ESSEX. It can—if it be carried cautiously. Yet not too
cautiously, but so that the news may fall opportunely, and seem
to get broken unawares. For the Queen hates the bearer of bad
tidings only less than the tidings itself.

LORD. What did he once say, " Fain would I climb, but that I
fear to fall! "

---

* Divina Natura agros dedit, ars humana ædificavit urbes. Varro:- De Re
Rustica.

ESSEX. And I say now, " Love lies in ambush where Ambition climbs! "

> Love lets one arrow fly
> Tipped with a glance and feathered with a sigh,
> And Pride will lay him down and die
> At the first blow—
> Take care!

Marry, love is a foolish thing!

Enter SIMKINS *with* WILKINS.

SIM. Nay, sir, love is a very serious thing, as my friend here has only learned in the last half hour.

WIL. It is like the plague—a man may take it lightly till it take him. And if it overtake him it will undertake him; for Love is a very undertaker to bury the gay in the grave.

SIM. He talks like a book.

ESSEX. In a shabby cover.

WIL. And without a title, my lords. But judge not a book by its cover, nor a man by his title—or lack of one. For Love, sirs, in this last half hour, has made me one of Nature's noblemen.

ESSEX. That's against Nature.

WIL. Sir, King Cupid can confer nobility on all men in half an hour.

ESSEX. 'Tis the way of all new nobility. It grows rank, like a mushroom bed.

WIL. Love, sir, can alter a man's habits quicker than he can change his clothes

Enter TOM, *who stands silent at back.*

TRIO.

(WILKINS, ESSEX, *and* SIMKINS.)

WIL. When a man is a lover, he's bound to discover
A fact of which I'm an informant:
His nature will change, or at least rearrange
Some points which were formerly dormant.

SIM. Perhaps more or less, in the matter of dress,
He was careless and shabbily shady;
But love will change that—he will buy a new hat,
When he's fallen in love with a lady!

ESSEX. For the love of a lady's a curious fact,
On a slovenly person it's certain to act;
If his coat is well brushed and his boots are well blacked,
You may know he's in love with a lady!

Though a small man by nature, your love will inflate your
   Proud heart to a size which is grander;
You'll feel you might rank (though a clerk in a bank)
   With a hero as brave as Lysander.
You'll be bursting with pluck, and will curse your ill-luck
   That while peacefully tied to a desk, you
Are longing to meet a mad dog in the street
   With some one or other to rescue!

WIL. Oh, the love of a lady has such an effect
Upon *me*, that I beg if you ever detect
A house that's on fire, or a ship that is wrecked,
   You'll allow me to fly to the rescue!

SIM. Then to live in an attic (on this be emphatic),
   An attic some lodging-house drab lets,
Is far happier if you share it with *her*,
   Than a palace. Put that on your tablets.

WIL. For your thoughts at all times you'll be breathing in
   rhymes,
   Though your friends never thought you a poet;
But if love blow its nose, it *can't* do it in prose,
   It *must* have a poet to blow it.
So the love of a lady's a curious thing,
A poetical fancy it's certain to bring,
And the present poetical song which I sing
   Is expressly intended to show it!

(Dance, and exeunt.)

Enter MAY QUEEN.

MAY Q. Well, where's your witch?
TOM. I know not that she is a witch.

MAY Q. I know she is. Contradiction is unmannerly.

TOM. But not unwomanly, so it seems.

MAY Q. Let me pass.

TOM. Am I in thy way?

MAY Q. Aye. I seem ever falling in with thee, for some
reason.

TOM. And falling out, for none. I'll go.

MAY Q. Stay, as thou *art* here. What character do you play
in the Morris Dance?

TOM. I'm put down for Robin Hood, your champion.

MAY Q. Nay; Robin Hood should be a man of quality, not
quantity.

Enter WILKINS.

Master Wilkins, will you play my Robin Hood to-day? And take
this man's part?

WIL. Aye, if he care not to fight for it.

TOM. Not I! [*Exit.*

WIL. I hate a coward! Ah! would that I could prove myself the hero love hath made me! If fierce fire would on a sudden leap from yonder castle, single handed I would scale the walls, and tearing down the burning masonry with frenzied fingers, fling the flaming fragments—fling the flaming fragments— Where would I fling the fragments?

Enter SIMKINS.

SIM. Upon the heads of the applauding crowd.

WIL. Aye.

SIM. Or if a mad bull, bursting from its barriers, bounded bellowing in our midst, with superhuman strength wouldst seize the snorting brute by head or tail and give him vigorous battle, though final victory—

WIL. Were a toss up! Aye!

SIM. Or if some gentle maid, a stranger, but a female in distress, flying from a murderous mob—

WIL. Would I protect her? Marry, that would I!

Enter JILL, *running. She clings to* WILKINS.

JILL. Save me!

SIM. This is your scene! I am in the audience.

Enter crowd, led by BUTCHER. *He seizes* JILL *and drags her to centre.*

JILL. Are you all cowards here?

WIL. No, not all, though I only answer for myself. (*Threatening the* BUTCHER.) Stand back!

BUTCHER. Stand back thyself! (*Boxes his ear.*)

WIL. Well, I will stand back; that's only fair. (*Retreating.*) A brave man cannot ask another to do what he dare not do himself. But fear not, gentle maid, I will protect thee from all harm.

MAY Q. She is a witch! Drown her!

ALL. Aye, a witch! A witch! (*They bind her arms.*)

WIL. A witch? Now that alters the complexion of the matter.

SIM. Your own altered somewhat. You grew very pale.

WIL. With anger. 'Tis the way of brave men. Oddsfish! if I stay here I shall fight the lot. I'd best away.

SIM. 'Tis the safest plan!

[*Exeunt.*

TOM *enters and* BEN.

JILL. I claim a hearing and fair trial!

Tom. And I claim that for her!

May Q. What right have you to speak for her?

Tom. The free right of a free man.

Essex *has entered.*

Essex. That's right enough. And I warrant these people say the same—or they wrong their own rights!

Soldier. Aye! Aye! Fair trial and no favour!

Essex. Untie her.

Jill (*to* Essex.) I thank you, sir.

Essex. Thank your champion here. (*To* Tom.) I do but say what the Queen would say—for she would love thy stock of courage as she loves the courage of thy stock. The Yeomen of England! She says they built her throne!

All. God save the Queen!

SONG.

Essex.

Who were the Yeomen, the Yeomen of England?
The free men were the Yeomen, the free men of England.
    Stout were the bows they bore
    When they went out to war.
Stouter their courage for the honour of England!

    And nations to Eastward,
    And nations to Westward,
        As foemen did curse them,
        The bowmen of England!
    No other land could nurse them,
    But their motherland, Old England!
And on her broad bosom did they ever thrive!

Where are the Yeomen, the Yeomen of England?
In homestead and cottage they still dwell in England!
    Stained with the ruddy tan
    God's air doth give a man,
Free as the winds that fan the broad breast of England!

    And nations to Eastward,
    And nations to Westward,
        As foemen may curse them,
        The Yeomen of England!
    No other land can nurse them,
    But their motherland, Old England!
And on her broad bosom shall they ever thrive!

Enter Wilkins.

Wil. Is the fighting finished?

SIM. It has not begun—yet. Stay, you'll have your chance

MAY Q. Let the witch have a trial—a witch's trial. Into the river with her! In with her!

TOM. Stay! I am a man of few words, but I would say as prettily as may be, if you will bear with my lack of fine language, that the first who lays finger on her I will kill.

MAY Q. So? Now, who's my champion?

SIM. (*to* WILKINS.) Your chance at last!

WIL. I will wait till last—'tis more modest. And modesty doth become a brave man.

SIM. I never saw a brave man become more modest!

BEN. I'll not fight my brother again. And besides and beyond and above, a Tailor is as big a man as a Forester—in his own way, so I've heard. (*Puts* TAILOR *in his place*.)

TAILOR. And a Butcher is as good a man as a Tailor—some-times. [*Exit.*

BUTCHER. And a Baker may talk louder than a Butcher—on occasion. [*Exit.*

BAKER. To say nothing of a Tinker. [*Exit.*

TINKER. Who hath nothing to say—at the moment. [*Exit.*

MAY Q. So much for my lovers! [*Exit.*

BEN. If it come to that—I'll fight. Though he pound me to a pudding.

WIL. And afterwards, *afterwards*, mind, when a pudding, you fight with *me*!

BEN. Who are you, small man?

WIL. The May Queen's champion, silkworm—her Robin Hood to-day! And through fire and water will I go for her to smile at me!

BEN. Into water shall you go forthwith—for her to laugh at you! Come, coxcomb!

[*He throws* WILKINS *into river, and exit.*

ESSEX (*to* JILL.) Why do you venture here if they hunt you as a witch?

JILL. 'Twas to carry this to a lady of the Court, whom I saw drop it in the forest. (*Showing paper.*)

ESSEX. This? (*Taking it.*)

JILL. Maybe she'll give me a soft word for it.

TOM. You would give your life for a soft word?

JILL. Perhaps, and get the best of the bargain.

TOM. Witch or no witch, and what you are I know not.

ESSEX. The Queen shall decide that—Queen Bess; I will bring you before her for judgment.

TOM. God save the Queen!

JILL. And me!

ESSEX (to LORD.) We are in luck's way! This is Raleigh's writing—a love-letter to Bessie Throckmorton! 'Tis an acrostic, hiding the name Bessie. Look—(Reading:)

> " Blessed the pen that writes my lady's name,
> " E'en tho' my pen do halt for very shame!
> " Shame at its own unworthiness to write .
> " So sweet a name—"

And so forth. Now mark how this will fall out for Raleigh. (To TOM.) This paper may be what she says, or it may be some witchcraft of her own; I know not—some love charm—

JILL. Sir, I declare—

ESSEX. The Queen shall judge. (To TOM.) Keep the girl in charge, and ask the Queen to judge her once for all. The Queen can do no wrong.

TOM. God save the Queen—and (to JILL) thee!

[Exeunt.

ESSEX. And Raleigh. He'll need all our prayers when the Queen reads this!

> (A March. The Crowd gathers. Then the Royal Barge
> approaches at back. QUEEN ELIZABETH enters from
> Barge, with BESSIE, and Ladies and Gentlemen of the
> Court. The Queen's Fool follows.)

CHORUS.

God save Elizabeth!
Sing with united breath
God save Elizabeth, and England bless!
May heaven prosper her!
May she our land prefer!
St. George for Merrie England and England's Queen Bess!

Long live Elizabeth!
Loyal and true till death
Unto Elizabeth shall England be!
Held high thy sceptre is
Over thine enemies!
Elizabeth for England, and England for thee!

SONG.—Elizabeth.

O peaceful England!
  While I my watch am keeping,
Thou, like Minerva,
  Weary of war, art sleeping!
Sleep on a little while,
And in thy slumber smile;
While thou art sleeping, I'll
  Be wakeful, ever wakeful!

Sword and buckler by thy side,
Rest on the shore of battle-tide,
  Which, like the ever-hungry sea,
  Roars round this Isle;
  Sleep till I awaken thee,
             smile;

England, fair England,
  Well hast thou earned thy slumber;
Yet, though thy bosom
  No breastplate now encumber,
Let not thy fingers yield
Grasp of thy sword and shield;
Thou shalt awake and wield
  Destruction when I call thee!

Sword and buckler laid aside,
Rest on the shore of battle-tide,
  Which, like the ever-hungry sea,
  Roars round this Isle;
  Sleep till I awaken thee,
  And in thy slumber smile!

Eliza. Where is Sir Walter Raleigh?

Essex. Where is Mistress Throckmorton?

Bess. Why question me, my lord?

Ral. (*entering.*) Because he would sooner question a woman than answer to a man. Cross swords and not questions, and I'll point my answers, I promise you! (*They draw.*)

Eliza. Put up your swords! What does this mean?

Bess. (*to* Elizabeth.) Why, Sir Walter loves *you*, madam, and the other is jealous.

Eliza. Put up your swords, gentlemen!

Ral. As I am a man, madam, I'll speak openly now of the love I have—

ELIZA. (*aside*.) As I am your Queen, be silent. I know of your love. Bessie has told me.

RAL. Bessie has told you?

ELIZA. Yes, and—I am not angry.

BESS. (*to* RALEIGH.) I have been falsely true and truly false, to save your life.

ELIZA. I'm in a merry mood. Where are the May Games? Let's see a Morris Dance! Who plays Robin Hood to-day?

SIM. Master Wilkins, your Grace, an actor of infinite dignity.

ELIZA. Well, where is he?

SIM. Madam, he comes.

Enter WILKINS, *from river, a miserable object.*

ELIZA. What's this? A joke—at my expense?

BEN enters

WIL. No, madam—at mine. Yet I count the cost nothing if it please you. (*To* BEN.) But you shall pay for it.

BEN. For his conceit I threw him—

WIL. As he says, madam, 'twas a quaint conceit of mine to be thrown into the river, that I might afterwards emerge in the character of Father Thames, whom I now represent. As Father Thames I stand before you as Ambassador for King Neptune, to offer unto Beauteous England the dignity and title of Mistress of the Sea!

ELIZA. A pretty conceit.

SIM (*to* BEN.) Marry, his conceit carries him further than you could throw him—into the Queen's favour.

SONG.

WILKINS, *with* CHORUS.

King Neptune sat on his lonely throne,
  On his lonely throne sat he;
King Neptune sat there all alone,
  As lonely as could be.
And he said, "Now who do you think would do
  To share my throne with me?"
And every fish, according to his wish,
  At once went out to see!

  At a nod
  From the god,
  All the Salmon and the Cod,
  And all the fish there be—
The Sturgeon and the Stickleback,

The Porpoise and the Conger Eel,
The Whitebait and the Octopus,
The Shark, the Mullet, and the Smelt,
The Brill, Anchovy, Sprat, and Plaice.
The Whale, the Winkle, and the Whelk,
The fish that coil and fish that fly,
The fish you boil and fish you fry,
The Turbot and the Mackerel,
The Lobster in the lobster-shell,
The Sole, the Whiting, and the Jell-
Y-fish, and more than I can tell—
Whose names I cannot speak or spell—
In fact, all fish fishmongers sell,
And all they do not sell as well—
In short, all fishes that do dwell
    Where Neptune bids them be,
      Away did swim
      To find for him
    A Mistress of the Sea!

King Neptune sat on his throne once more.
  On his throne once more sat he,
When the fish came back from England's shore.
  And clapped their fins with glee.
For they said, " We've seen the fairest Queen
  That in the world can be!"
And Neptune saith, " That's Queen Elizabeth!
  And she's the Queen for me!"

    Is it odd
    That the god
  Told the Salmon and the Cod
    To publish this decree?
The Sturgeon and the Stickleback,
The Porpoise and the Conger Eel,
The Whitebait and the Octopus,
The Shark, the Mullet, and the Smelt,
The Brill, Anchovy, Sprat, and Plaice.
The Whale, the Winkle, and the Whelk,
The fish that coil and fish that fly,
The fish you boil and fish you fry,
The Turbot and the Mackerel,
The Lobster in the lobster-shell,
The Sole, the Whiting, and the Jell-
Y-fish, and more than I can tell—
Whose names I cannot speak or spell—
In fact, all fish fishmongers sell,
And all they do not sell as well—

All such as in the sea do dwell,
Did publish this decree,
That Beauteous Bess
All men address
As Mistress of the Sea!

ELIZA. 'Tis a quaint conceit!

WIL. Anon I play Robin Hood in the Morris Dance; and later I would provide for your delight a certain Masque of St. George and the Dragon, in which I play St. George, and my friend here the Dragon, whom I beat unmercifully and finally slay— (*indicating* BEN)—if it be your pleasure?

ELIZA. We'll see it. Bring your May Queen now, with her Court of Robin Hood, Tom the Piper, Friar Tuck, and all. Ho, a Morris Dance!

WIL. As your Grace commands.   [*Exit.*

ELIZA. I love the old tales of Robin Hood. Bessie, do you remember how the song goes Maid Marion sings?

BESS. Yes, madam, I was reminded of it to-day.

ELIZA. Let's hear it.

FINALE.

BESS.   It is a tale of Robin Hood,
                Of Tuck and Little John,
          And all of those who followed him,
                With his Maid Marion.
          For she followed him
                Beneath the greenwood tree,
                As Love may follow thee!
                   Though Fortune frown,
                   Thou'lt wear a crown
                A king may never see!
                   With a hey, Jolly Robin!

          Then who would not be out of Court,
                As Robin Hood befell,
          To fare as Love may bid him fare,
                And bid all else farewell?
          If Love follow him
                Beneath the greenwood tree,
                As Love may follow thee,
                   Though Fortune frown,
                   Thou'lt wear a crown
                A king may never see!
                   With a hey, Jolly Robin!

ELIZA. Would queens could love as Marion did! Heigho!

ESSEX. Would I were Robin Hood if that were so!

Enter with Tom & Jill

Tom *enters, bringing on* Jill.

TOM.　　Madam, I ask a favour! I plead the cause
　　　　Of a poor sorely-stricken girl, whom folk
　　　　Do call Jill-all-alone—

MAY Q.　　　　　　　　She is a witch!

TOWNSPEOPLE.
　　　　　　Aye! Aye! A witch! She is a witch! A witch!
　　　　A witch! A witch!

ELIZA.　　　　　　　Who speak against her?

MAY Q.　　　　　　　These
　　　　Four worthy citizens of Windsor Town!
　　　　(*The* BUTCHER, BAKER, TINKER, *and* TAILOR *advance.*)

QUARTET.

　　　　We are four men of Windsor—
　　　　A Butcher of Windsor,
　　　　And a Baker of Windsor,
　　　　And a Tinker of Windsor,
　　　　And a Tailor of Windsor.
　　　　　　And good meat I sell,
　　　　　　　And good bread I bake,
　　　　　　And my tin is good tin,
　　　　　　　And good clothes I make!
　　　　So we all ply a good trade in Windsor,
　　　　　　　And cry—
　　　　Who'll buy? Who'll buy? Who'll **buy—buy—buy**
　　　　　From the four men of Windsor?
　　　　　The Butcher of Windsor,
　　　　　And the Baker of Windsor,
　　　　　And the Tinker of Windsor,
　　　　　And the Tailor of Windsor.
　　　　When you buy meat try *my* meat!
　　　　When you buy bread try *my* bread!
　　　　When you buy tin try *my* tin!
　　　　When you buy clothes try *my* clothes!
　　　　For we all ply a good trade in Windsor,
　　　　　　　And cry—
　　　　Who'll buy? Who'll buy? Who'll **buy—buy—buy**
　　　　　From the four men of Windsor?

ELIZA. (*to* JILL.)　　　　What say you, girl?
　　　　They say you are a witch!

JILL.　　　　　　　　　　A witch is wise:
　　　　So if a witch I should know more than they:
　　　　But if I am a witch I know much less,
　　　　Because I do not know I am a witch;
　　　　But I do know what I do know! Now, hark!

I know that love
Is far above
    All other pretty things:
And I do know
That being so
    'Tis coveted by kings.
    But love hath wings
And passeth by
A king sometimes for such as I!
I wonder why?

CONCERTED PIECE.

MAY Q.   By those words I accuse her
          Of drawing by her magic
          The love of faithful lovers
          Unto herself by witchcraft!

ESSEX.   She had this piece of writing,
          Which I did find upon her—
          Perhaps it is a love charm,
          A thing of evil purpose.
                (He hands RALEIGH'S *verses to* ELIZABETH.)

                Enter RALEIGH

ELIZA.   The verse is an acrostic,
          And its initial letters
          Do make the name of " Bessie,"
          And I do know the writing.

ESSEX.   Why, 'tis Sir Walter Raleigh's!

ELIZA.   Yes; is it not thy writing?
          And *my* name that is written?

RAL.   The writing is my writing,
          And I give back the letter
          To her for whom I wrote it.
             (He gives the paper to BESSIE THROCKMORTON.)

ALL.   Bessie   Throckmorton!

ENSEMBLE.

RAL   My troth is plighted
            To this gentle maid;
          In secret I have paid
            My past addresses!
              Blow high, blow low!
              Now *coram publico*,
            I let the whole world know
          My heart is Bessie's!

Bess.	Though I'm affrighted, And sore afraid, Though dread of her tirade My soul possesses! Blow high, blow low! However fortune blow, I'll let the whole world go For thy caresses!
Eliza.	Now I am slighted For another maid! Love's like a falcon strayed With broken jesses! Fly high, fly low, Wherever love may go, What lure can woman throw For lost caresses!
Chorus.	In love united They are not afraid! In secret has he paid His past addresses! Blow high, blow low, However fortune blow, He'll let the whole world go For her caresses!

SOLO.

Jill.

Jill.	I know that love Is far above All jewels that are seen: And I do know That being so 'Tis wanted by a Queen. But Love, I ween, May pass her by— So I may laugh,
Eliza.	No! Thou shalt die! (*A Soldier seizes* Jill.) Go—lodge this witch within the Castle walls; I'll see her burn there! Thou, Sir Walter, Go to thy country house and banishment. (*To* Bessie.) Go to the Castle, thou—a prisoner!

[*Exit* Elizabeth, *in a rage, with* Essex *and Ladies* Jill
is dragged off by Soldier.

DUET.

RALEIGH *and* BESSIE.

RAL.   BESS.

Be not affrighted!   Though I'm affrighted,
Sweet, be not afraid!   And sore afraid!
Although the Queen's tirade   Though dread of her tirade
 Thy soul oppresses!   My soul possesses!
  Blow high, blow low,   Blow high, blow low,
  However fortune blow,   However fortune blow,
   I'll let the whole world go   I'll let the whole world go
For thy caresses!   For thy caresses!

(As the lovers are parting, the Morris Dancers are heard approaching. The Queen's Fool runs across to RALEIGH *and* BESSIE, *and bids them listen to*

THE SONG OF THE MORRIS DANCERS.

If Love follow thee
  Beneath the greenwood tree,
   Though Fortune frown,
   Thou'lt wear a crown
A king may never see!
   With a hey, Jolly Robin!

The Morris Dancers enter to the refrain of their song, led by WILKINS *in the character of Robin Hood.* RALEIGH *embraces* BESSIE, *and exit.* QUEEN ELIZABETH *re-enters with* ESSEX *and others. As she is passing up to her barge, she sees* BESSIE, *who is standing looking after her lover.* ESSEX *beckons a Man-at-arms, who goes to* BESSIE. *The* QUEEN *goes up to the barge, and is standing on it looking back at* BESSIE, *who is escorted up as the Morris Dancers form their group of " Robin Hood's Wedding," and the*

CURTAIN FALLS

ACT II.

SCENE.—*A glade in Windsor Forest.* "*Herne's Oak,*" R.C. *JILL is discovered tending a small fire of sticks, over which hangs a cooking-pot. She listens to voices heard singing in the distance.*

CHORUS (*heard in distance off.*)

The month o' May has come to-day,
 And who will wear a frown-a?
For where's the knave
 Who'll not be merry?
We'll dig his grave,
 With a derry down derry,
A down, a down, a down-a!

SOLO.

JILL. Cat, cat, where have you been?
I've been to the Castle to look at the Queen
Cat, cat, did she sit on a throne?
Verily, yes, like a Jill-all-alone.

Cat, cat, what do you mean?
A Queen is a woman, a woman a Queen!
Cat, cat, shall I sit on a throne?
Verily, yes, when a lover you own.

CHORUS (*heard off*).

The Queen o' May is crowned to-day
 With a crown, a crown, a crown-a!
Then where's the knave
 Who'll not be merry?
And join the stave,
 With a derry down derry,
A down, a down, a down-a!

(JILL *listens, then removes tripod, treads out the fire, and hides in the hollow oak.*)

Enter TOM *and* BEN.

BEN. What did you find at the Castle?

TOM. Sentries on every gate to keep Raleigh out, and his lady in.

BEN. And your witch?

TOM. She is to burn at sunset.

(JILL *comes from oak.*)

BEN. Look!

TOM. (*to* JILL.) How did you escape?

JILL. By witchcraft—if I'm a witch!

BEN. So I thought—we'll take her back; 'tis the Queen's service. (*Takes* JILL *by the wrist.*)

TOM. If she confess herself a witch—

Enter BESSIE *from oak.*

BESS. (*entering.*) Stay! She has saved my life!

BEN. By witchcraft?

BESS. No, by her knowledge of a certain passage from the Castle which leads by a secret trap-door out of Herne's Oak there. She is no witch.

JILL. I prayed you keep in hiding, and have a care.

BESS. I have cares enough, without caring to see care come to others for want of a little understanding.

JILL. (*to Tom.*) Well, it's true enough. You know now why Herne's Oak is haunted. I had the secret from my grandfather. He guarded the passage for King Harry, who sometimes used it. Within there still hang the hunting horn and the deerskin with antlers with which he sometimes raised the appearance of Herne the Hunter. It kept gossips from the place, as it might do again.

BEN. Why did King Harry want a secret passage?

JILL. I know not—but England's a free country.

BESS. And Harry was a free liver.

TOM. Not to say a free lover.

JILL. Yet he was married in his time, they tell me.

QUARTET.

BESSIE, JILL, TOM, *and* BEN.

In England, merrie England,
    There lived a king upon a time—
    To tell his name might be a crime—
In England, merrie England!
    But he sometimes did doff his crown,
    And walk abroad like any clown,
In England, merrie England!
    And if he met a pretty wench,
    And maids are fairer than the French,
In England, merrie England,
    He'd kiss her, as an Englishman
    Should kiss a maiden when he can,
In England, merrie England!

So let us sing,
God save the King
Of England, merrie England!
With fal la lal,
For bluff King Hal
Of England, merrie England!

[*Exeunt* Tom *and* Ben, r. Bessie *to Oak, with* Jill.
Enter Chorus of Men, with Simkins, *the* Butcher, *and the*
Tailor, *singing.*

TRIO AND CHORUS.

Tailor. The sun in the heaven is high!
No clouds do bespeckle the sky!
And a man and a maid
Do kiss in the shade—
And so shall my bottle and I!
With a hey, and a ho,
And a hey nonny no,
A fig for the weather, say I!

Chorus. For in summer or winter,
In autumn or spring,
Whatever betide me—
Whatever they bring,
With my bottle beside me
I'm able to sing
My hey nonny, hey nonny no!

Simkins. The clouds they may come in the sky!
The rain it may fall by-and-bye!
And the water may drench
The man and the wench—
A fig for cold water, say I!
With a hey, and a ho,
And a hey nonny no,
Whatever the weather, I'm dry!

Chorus. For in summer or winter,
In autumn or spring, &c.

Butcher. The snow it may cover the ground!
The river with ice may be bound!
But when maidens grow old,
And love groweth cold,
My bottle and I shall be found!
With a hey, and a ho,
And a hey nonny no,
However the seasons come round!

Chorus. For in summer or winter,
In autumn or spring, &c.

Enter WILKINS, *with the* TINKER *and the* BAKER.

WILKINS. Now the business of the day stands thus. First, we meet here, by Herne's Oak, and arrange the music play of Robin Hood's meeting with Little John—very proper to be played in the May Games, in which I play Robin Hood.

SIMKINS. And I, the Friar.

WILKINS. Then having perfected ourselves in our parts, we proceed to the Castle to play before the Queen's servants. But— and mark this "but"—if we do meet the Queen by the way, we forthwith commence my Masque of St. George and the Dragon. (*Showing manuscript.*)

SIM. In which I play the part of the Dragon.

WIL. The hind part of the Dragon.

TINKER. And what do I play?

BUTCHER. And I?

BAKER. And I?

TAILOR. And I?

WIL. You play the music.

SIM. Is the masque musical?

WIL. Yes. It hath parts in it for the drum, tabor, sackbut, Jew's harp, and voice. Of these, the drum sets the time, the sackbut sets the tune—

SIM. Will you give me the sackbut, to set the tune?

WIL. I would give you the sackbut you set the scenes.

SIM. How many kinds of music are there?

WIL. Why, two kinds. Instrumental, when there are no words; and vocal, or singing, when there is language applied.

SIM. If I sing, what language will be applied to the music?

WIL. I know not. But be advised, and sing only to the deaf and dumb, for a charity.

SIM. Why should I sing for a charity?

WIL. Because charity suffereth long. And they who suffer long muzzle their dogs, so that they cannot howl. Which is sound sense, though it sounds nonsense. For music is, in a sense, a sense of sound. And if your senses be sound, you will make music which hath tunes in it, and so give airs to your listeners, as is proper. But if your senses be not sound, you will make music which hath no tune in it, and give yourself airs, and call it opera, which is properer. But for myself, give me a tune which a man may hum an he please, or whistle an he please, or step to an he please, and straightforward withal, not sideways or round the corner like a bumble-bee in a bottle-neck—

SIM. I know such a tune.   One that long ago took root in my mind.   I'll uproot it.

WIL. Nay.   Let it stay there, lest some of the soil come with it. If you have an ear for fine music, listen to me.

DUET.

WILKINS *and* SIMKINS.

WIL.
I may be wrong,
But I long for a song
    With a tune that a man may march to!
That will make you shout
When you feel " washed out,"
    And your courage will lend some starch to!
Of course I know
Such a taste is low,
    But there's many a mind may plumb it,
But what on Earth
Can be the worth
    Of a tune if a man can't hum it?

Then, come, come,
Follow the drum,
    Tho' its music mayn't be grand!
Tho' the words be Dutch
Let the tune be such
    As a Briton can understand!
And whether it be
A song of the sea,
    Or a lay of the good dry land,
Let Art go hang,
If the tune go "bang!"
    When it's played on a big brass band!

SIM.
So nowadays
Our musical plays
    Should be very peculiar salads
Of simple sounds
From " merry-go-rounds,"
    With occasional third-rate ballads!

And if these you mix
With big drum sticks
    (And serve with a big brass ladle).
Little critical boys
Will applaud your noise
    As soon as they leave the cradle !

Singing, Come, come,
Follow the drum,
    Tho' the music mayn't be grand !
Tho' the words be Dutch
Let the tune be such
    As a baby can understand !
And whether it be
A song of the sea,
    Or a lay of the good dry land,
Let Art go hang,
If the tune go " bang ! "
    When it's played on a big brass band !

Enter Page, with the Fool, who is disguised as an Apothecary.

PAGE. Out of the way, clowns ! The Queen comes !

WIL. The Queen, sir? (*Opening manuscript of Masque.*)

PAGE. Aye ! Begone ! (*To Apothecary.*) Wait there !

WIL. Out of sight ! But be ready to spring out upon the Queen with the Prologue of the Seven Champions of Christendom when I give the cue.

SIM. What's the cue?

WIL. " God save the Queen ! " Begone ! I'll wait here.
                                  [*Exeunt others.*

PAGE. Why do you loiter?

WIL. Why, sir—

PAGE. Dost ask me why? Because I prefer thy disappear-ance to thine appearance, and I like not thy proximity.

WIL. Judge not a man by the outward appearance of his proximity, young sir. As for my proximity, 'tis a flesh and blood proximity, with two eyes, a nose, and a mouth—the same as thine own. And when next you find fault with a man's face, call it a face and not a proximity; for some men understand not the French language as *I* do !

    Enter QUEEN ELIZABETH, *with Lady-in-Waiting, and second Page, and a Lord.*

ELIZA. Where's Essex? I said I'd meet him here.

PAGE. Here's the apothecary, madam, of whom he told you.

ELIZA. Ah! (*To others.*) Go, and wait near. I'll talk to this apothecary alone. They tell me he is cunning with his drugs, and my physicians cannot comprehend what ails me to-day.

LORD. I can. 'Tis an affection of the heart.

LADY. Complicated with the black humour of jealousy. There's nought more dangerous.

LORD. To others! Bessie Throckmorton is like to die of it.
[*Exeunt.*

ELIZA (*to Fool.*) Come hither! (*To Pages.*) Go!

SECOND PAGE. I like not to leave your Grace with this knave.

ELIZA. You are a grave boy, and a brave boy, and a pretty boy, and (*she kisses him*) a faithful sweetheart. Now go!

SECOND PAGE. If I were ten years older I'd marry her.

FIRST PAGE. If she were ten years younger, I'd do it.

ELIZA. Now. You looked starved, Apothecary! [*Exeunt.*

FOOL. Yes, madam. 'Tis a poor life to live on drugs.

Enter WILKINS, with others.

WIL. God save the Queen!

ELIZA. Who are you, fellow?

WILKINS. St. George of England, madam! And I have with me St. Denis of France, St. James of Spain, St. Anthony of Italy—

ELIZA. Enough!

WIL. Then there are more than enough, for there are three more. St. Patrick of Ireland, St. Andrew of—

ELIZA. Peace, fool! I'm in no mood for fooling. I'll listen to thee anon—perhaps.

WIL. Anon!

BUTCHER (*and others.*) Anon! Anon! [*Exeunt.*

ELIZA. (*to Fool.*) So you live a poor life? What would you give for an hundred crowns?

FOOL. Why, madam, my poor life—if it were worth the money, which it cannot be, seeing that if I give up living 'twill not be for money, but the want of it.

ELIZA. Listen! I need a drug that deals death, not life. A drug that's swift and secret. One that counterfeits some natural disease in Nature's armoury. A drug that strikes like a dagger, but leaves no pommel in the wound, to point suspicion. Know you such a drug?

FOOL. I could concoct it. Is it for a man or a woman?

ELIZA. Give me enough for a man.

FOOL. 'Twill be less than for a woman.

ELIZA. How so?

FOOL. Why, thus—the first and last effect of such a drug is loss of breath. And the first and last effect of loss of breath is loss of speech. And 'tis easier to stay a man's speech than a woman's.

ELIZA. Stay thine, and bring me the drug.

FOOL. In an hour, madam.

ELIZA. Here!

[*Exit.*

Enter RALEIGH, *dressed as a Forester, and with his beard shaved.*

RAL. Listen, knave! Deliver not that drug to the Queen, as you value your own life! I am Sir Walter Raleigh.

FOOL. Then you are a bare-faced impostor, and I a bearded one! Look! (*He takes off his false beard and opens his cloak, showing his motley.*)

RAL. The Queen's Fool!

FOOL. Aye—more fool than knave; and not the first fool that disguised his folly to some good purpose. Fear not, Walter! Your sweetheart shall live to die of worse medicine than mine! You have a fool for a friend, which is better than a wise man for an enemy. Therefore rejoice, if for nought else. Anon, gossip! (*Exit.*)

(RALEIGH *turns and sees* JILL, *who has entered.*)

RAL. (*to* JILL.) Tell me, girl—do you know where the Morris dancers are?

JILL. On their way to the Castle, to play before the Royal servants.

RAL. And I would join them—'tis my way into the Castle.

JILL. Then you'll be of Robin Hood's merry men—and your looks belie you, for you do not look merry.

RAL. I am the most miserable of men; for I am in love and outlaw!

JILL. Then you are in the best and out of the worst in the world—Love and the Law! So you should be merry, like Robin Hood.

RAL. But " Love followed him."

JILL. " As love may follow thee "—it may, sir, it may. Is not this the month of May? Come, let your brown thoughts take a lesson from the bees. Look! They do not loiter where there are no sweets, but suck honey where they can. 'Tis the wise way, or I'm no witch!

DUET.

JILL and RALEIGH.

It is the merry month of May.
The bees do hum a roundelay,
        And all the world is sunny.
So let your brown thoughts hie away,
        And search the world for honey.

Oh, love, it is a happy thing,
It cometh unto clown or king,
        As any one may see.
And of all places where it flies,
There is no place beneath the skies
More fair than where the bracken grows,
The honeysuckle and the rose,
        Beneath the greenwood tree.
While bees do hum their roundelay,
'Tis there I'll dream that Love some day
        May even come to me.   [*Exeunt.*

Enter Chorus, with QUEEN OF THE MAY, *&c.*

CHORUS.   The Queen o' May is crowned to-day
                With a crown, a crown, a crown-a!
            Then where's the knave
                Who'll not be merry?
            We'll dig his grave,
                With a derry down derry,
            A down, a down, a down-a.

MAY Q.   Now what is a good thing
                For Jack and for Jill?

CHORUS.   A song is a good thing!

MAY Q.   Who'll sing one?

CHORUS.   I will!

MAY Q.   Then sing it, sing it, sing it,
                When it's the Queen's will!
            But what is a good thing
                For Jack and for Jill?

CHORUS.   A kiss is a good thing!

MAY Q.   Who'll kiss me?

CHORUS.   I will!

MAY Q.   Then kiss me, kiss me, kiss me,
                When it is the Queen's will!

> But what is a good thing
> For Jack and for Jill?

CHORUS. A dance is a good thing!

MAY Q. Who'll dance one?

CHORUS. I will!

MAY Q. Then trip it, trip it, trip it,
For it is the Queen's will!

(Dance.)

Enter RALEIGH.

RAL. Queen of the May, I ask a favour of you.

TINKER. How now! Do you think she will favour strangers when there are men of Windsor—

MAY Q. Ask on.

RAL. It is that I may join your Morris dancers when they enter the Castle, ~~and so enter it with them.~~

MAY Q. We go there anon to play Robin Hood.

RAL. Let me play a character. I know all the old games, words and music. Let me go too.

TAILOR. ~~Aye, go to! go to! Look you—~~

MAY Q. You shall go. In what character?

RAL. 'Twill be in the character of a lover, however you care to call me.

BUTCHER. Who are you who talk so loud of lover? There are enough men in Windsor to make her a husband, if she would but take one of us.

RAL. Good sooth, sir, I am no lover of this maid; but there is a sweet maid in the Castle—

MAY Q. So? There is a sweet maid in the Castle—and am I so sour?

RAL. Nay, I doubt not you are fair and sweet as you are sweetly fair—a very English rose. There is no sweeter flower in all Cupid's garden.

SONG.

RALEIGH.

> Dan Cupid hath a garden
> Where women are the flow'rs;
> And lovers' laughs and lovers' tears
> The sunshine and the show'rs.
> And oh, the sweetest blossom
> That in his garden grows,
> The fairest queen, it is, I ween,
> The perfect English rose!

Let others make a garland
    Of every flow'r that blows,
But I will wait till I may pluck
    My dainty English rose!
In perfume, grace, and beauty
    The rose doth stand apart—
God grant that I, before I die,
    May wear one on my heart!

Enter Wilkins.

Wil. Harkee, sirrah! Do you sing the praises of this maid? Or do you prefer another maid above this maid?

Ral. Why?

Wil. Why—I am her Robin Hood. And if you prefer this maid to another, I beat you on my own account for your offence. But if you prefer another maid to this maid, I beat you on her account for her defence. Which you will, so we fight.

Ral. Give me a quarter-staff!

Wil. Nay! I spoke but to prove your courage! I like a man who'll take a broken head for the sake of his lady. You are welcome to your own opinion—I will not take it from you.

Ral. Thanks, friend!

Enter Tom.

Tom. Hearken to me! I love the maid they call Jill-all-alone, I say she is no witch, and I would have had her chosen Queen of the May for Windsor.

May Q. (*to* Wilkins.) You heard that?

Wil. No. I am a thought deaf in the right ear.

Tom. I love Jill-all-alone. She is no witch, and I would she had been chosen Queen of the May for Windsor.

May Q. Will you let him say that?

Wil. He has said it, and that can't be helped. But I assuredly shall not let him say it again.

Tom. I love Jill-all-alone. I would she had been chosen Queen of the May for Windsor.

May Q. He hath said it again.

Wil. He hath.

Ral. A direct challenge, friend.

Wil. Yes; I must beat him. (*Preparing to fight, then hesitating.*) Stay! This Jill-all-alone is a witch, therefore he is bewitched. Therefore it is not his fault, and a man must not be punished for what is not a fault. Therefore go your ways, and take a treacle posset; I'll not harm thee.

TOM. Do you forget we are to play the first meeting of Robin Hood and Little John—where they fight; and I play Little John, who thrashes Robin Hood?

WIL. I did not remember—at the moment—that you played Little John.

RAL. (*to* WILKINS.) Let me play your part!

WIL. You? Why, sir, why? Can you give me any reason that you should? (*Aside.*) Try to think, sir, and I'll owe you a new crown for the cracked one you'll get. (*Aloud.*) Is there any reason why I should give up my place to you?

RAL. Only this—I am Sir Walter Raleigh.

ALL. Sir Walter!

RAL. And I would take any part which will take me into the Castle to take the part of my lady, who is in sore distress.

WIL. Say no more, sir, say no more! There's reason enough. The part is yours. You shall play Robin Hood and be thrashed by Little John, while I play the Friar.

SIM. And what of me?

WIL. You shall content yourself with the hind legs of the Dragon. But now for Robin Hood and Little John, and to see what shape we make.

THE PLAY OF ROBIN HOOD AND LITTLE JOHN.

WIL.   Two merry men a-drinking, a-drinking!

RAL.   Before the moon was sinking, a-sinking!

TOM.   A Stranger he did pass that way,
          And he did listen to their lay—

ALL.   All on a summer's night!

RAL.   Who dares to drink
                  Or fight with me?
              I'll not shrink
                  Whoever he be!
                  I'll crack his crown
                  Or drink him down
                      Before the grey of morning!

WIL.   As Robin lay a-thinking, a-thinking—

RAL.   And Tuck did sit a-drinking, a-drinking—

TOM.   The Stranger he did stoutly say,
          This is a game that *two* can play—

ALL.   All on a summer's night!

WIL.   Then Tuck he stood a-blinking, a-blinking,
At Robin Hood a-winking, a-winking,
And Tuck did to the Stranger say,
" To Robin Hood there's toll to pay,"

ALL.   All on a summer's night!

(*The Fight.*)

RAL.   Poor Robin lay a-thinking, a-thinking—

WIL.   And Tuck he sat a-blinking, a-blinking—

TOM.   And Little John did sing this lay,
For he it was who won the day—

ALL.   All on a summer's night!

TOM.   Who dares to drink
Or fight with me?
I'll not shrink,
Whoever he be.
I'll crack his crown
Or drink him down
Before the grey of morning.

ALL   Then all did sit a-drinking, a-drinking,
Until the moon was sinking, a-sinking,
For Little John did with them stay,
So all did sing this roundelay
On many a summer's night!

Who dares to drink, &c.

WIL. (to RALEIGH.) Well, sir, you shall play the part, and as for me, I'll content myself with the two characters of St. George and the King of Egypt which I play in my Masque. Now to the Castle, unless we meet the Queen by the way, when she may insist upon my Masque immediately.

ALL. To the Castle!

RAL. To my lady!   [*Exeunt all to reprise.*

Enter JILL, *followed by* BESSIE, *from Herne's Oak.*

JILL. Wait here, lady. I'll run and bring your lover.

BESS. I am afraid! I thought I heard footsteps in the passage, following.

JILL. 'The echo. I'll bring your lover—he'll kiss your colour back, I warrant.

BESS. Thou art a kind girl!

JILL. Nay! But we are two of a kind. For we both carry our lives in our hands, and love in our hearts.

BESS. A double burden.

JILL. Aye! But what's one without the other?   I have heard it said—

> " Life's a chime, and Love the ringer;
> Life's a lute, and Love the singer;
>> Though he choose a song of sadness,
>> 'Tis a song to heed."

Anon, lady! I'll run!

[Exit.

BESS. Aye! 'Tis a song to heed!

SONG.

BESSIE.

> Who shall say that Love is cruel?
> I do guard it as a jewel,
>> Counting it the single flower
>> In a world of weed!
> What if Love do bring me sorrow?
> Love to-day and die to-morrow—
>> Loveless life is lifeless living—
>> That were death indeed!
> Life is sweet, but Love is sweeter;
> Life is prose—but Love a metre,
>> Throbbing with the pulse of music—
>> All that lovers need.

> Life's a chime, and Love the ringer;
> Life's a lute, and Love the singer;
>> Though he choose a song of sadness,
>> 'Tis a song to heed.

> Loveless life is lifeless living,
> Only Love hath power of giving
>> Unto life its breath and beauty—
>> Love is all divine.
> Life's the canvas—nought is duller,
> Till it gloweth gay with colour,
>> 'Neath the hand of Love the painter,
>> Master of Design!
> Life's the parchment—but the sonnet
> Only Love can write upon it.
>> Life is but an empty goblet,
>> Love's the rosy wine.

> Life's a chime, and Love the ringer;
> Life's a lute, and Love the singer;
>> Though he sing a song of sadness,
>> I will not repine.

Enter JILL, *followed by* RALEIGH.

JILL (*to* BESS.) Mistress, look up! It is your lover
RAL. Love has followed me—
BESS. Beneath the greenwood tree!

Enter ESSEX *from Herne's Oak.*

ESSEX. And so have I!
RAL. You!
BESS. You followed me—
ESSEX. Being free, and you a prisoner, I took that liberty.
RAL. (*clapping his hand to his hip.*) I have no sword! I'd
give my right hand for a sword.
ESSEX. A bargain! Take mine, and I take your hand! For
we are friends—by circumstance.
BESS. I do not understand.
RAL. Nor I!
ESSEX. You understand the game of chess—I have often seen
you play with the Queen. (*To* BESSIE.) Do not sigh, that is
over; and it is I who am playing now—
RAL. A crooked game?
ESSEX. A knight's move. And the stake is—a golden crown.
Now, watch the board. I have a mind to take the queen—she is
guarded by another knight—you! But a pawn may take a
knight—a pretty pawn in petticoats. And if you be taken, I
may take the queen. The pawn moves, is then stopped by a
castle, then breaks out, and the knight is taken; he is off the
board, and out of my way. I take the queen, a bishop comes
up, and—mate! I've won a crown.
RAL. In other words—
ESSEX. In plain words, I would have you married—to any one
but the Queen. I followed this lady's escape with interest; and
if you will follow my advice, I'll wager a crown on two things—
that you marry the sweetest maid in England and I marry
Elizabeth.
RAL. Then—we are friends—by circumstance. What would
you have us do?
ESSEX. Watch me—I meet the Queen here anon. Leave pro-
jects to me, and me to this project—that a crown weighs more
than Cupid, nowadays.
BESS. Not always. There are still love matches in the world.
ESSEX. They're matches that will never set the Thames a-fire
Love's no longer a baby; he has grown up and turned shopkeeper

SONG.

ESSEX, *with* BESSIE, JILL, *and* RALEIGH.

When Cupid first this old world trod,
He was, you know, a baby god;
And old Dame Nature nursed the lad,
But let him run about unclad.
One day my Lady Fashion came,
And blushed beneath her rouge with shame
To see the pretty innocent
Unclothed, in Gipsy Nature's tent.

> And, heedless of Dame Nature's curse,
> She took him from his gipsy nurse,
> And set him in her chariot,
> Determined to improve his lot.

Beneath my Lady Fashion's rule,
Poor Cupid then was sent to school,
And learned the laws of common-sense,
And how to value pounds and pence.
She dressed him up from toe to top,
And put him in a London shop,
Where Cupid, at the counter, sells
New tunes for modern marriage bells.

> For Love no longer baits his hooks
> With gentle sighs and tender looks,
> But nowadays poor lovers get
> Entangled by a million (nett!).

So Cupid seldom comes to us
In puris naturalibus,
For such extremely simple guise
Would shock the modern worldly wise.
Yet even now sometimes, they say,
He takes a little holiday;
And every now and then returns
Where old Dame Nature waits, and yearns!

> For Love's a gipsy still at heart,
> Though fashion makes him look so smart;
> And I, for one, would not complain
> Were he a naked child again!

[*Exeunt* BESSIE *and* RALEIGH.

JILL. Sir, you have learnt the secret way by which to escape
from the Castle. You will tell no one—not even the Queen?

ESSEX. As I mean to be her husband, I swear it! Now listen,
a Roland for an Oliver; do you help me in a plan to work upon

the Queen's tears for her benefit and theirs—and thine own. Let thy long lover don the deer-skin dress which hangs in the passage—if he would save thy life—and we'll prick the Queen's conscience to pity, with an apparition of Herne the Hunter! Sound the hunting horn twice or thrice, and—hush!

JILL. I'll see to it!   [*Exit to oak.*

Enter WILKINS.

WIL. Pray, sir, does the Queen come this way?

ESSEX. What matter is it of yours?

WIL. The small matter of the matter of a Masque of St. George and the Dragon, which I have prepared for the Queen's pleasure, if it please her, and fall in with her plans—

ESSEX. It may fall in with mine. I'll see she sees it. Is it a good Masque?

WIL. Sir, Shakespeare never wrote anything quite like it.

ESSEX. Good!

WIL. Very good, sir!

Enter JILL.

ESSEX (*to* JILL.) Come with me, and lend me your aid, and you—(*to* WILKINS)—see that you arrange this with the players. (*He whispers.*)

WIL. (*his expression changes.*) And you say that if we play such a prank upon the Queen we shall be playing for the Queen's benefit?

ESSEX. Yes.

WIL. I'd rather the Queen played for mine. But I'll see to it.

ESSEX (*to* JILL.) Come! (*To* WILKINS.) Anon!

WIL. Anon, sir, anon!

Enter BEN *and* SIMKINS.

SIM. Concerning the Dragon which we play—

WIL. You understand the purport of the Masque. The King of Egypt hath a daughter who is to be sacrificed to the Dragon.

BEN. And I play the legs of the Dragon.

WIL. The forelegs. And you—(*to* SIMKINS)—the hind part. So! (*Putting them in position*).

SIM. Why should I suffer myself to play the tail to his head?

WIL. To save thyself suffering. The front part is the part I beat in the fight.

BEN. Why should I play the part you beat?

WIL. Why, man, 'tis the better part—the head part—the thinking part—the part of intellect.

BEN. Doth a Dragon think with his intellect?

WIL. More than with his tail. Now, the Dragon comes after the Princess to devour her.

SIM. And do you come after the Dragon?

WIL. No. I come first, and challenge Dragons, all and sundry. And then this Dragon comes forth.

SIM. And do other Dragons come second and third?

WIL. There are no other Dragons.

BEN. And what am I?

WIL. The forelegs of the Dragon.

SIM. How many legs hath a Dragon?

WIL. A Dragon hath four legs, the same as any other centipede.

BEN. Then I am all its legs?

WIL. No, no! 'Tis clear enough! It hath four legs, and two legs are forelegs, so with its hind legs it is four-legged; and it comes forth before me after I come, as I have come after it, being forewarned, and therefore forearmed.

SIM. Then it is four-armed as well as four-legged?

WIL. It is I who am forearmed. It hath no arms but its teeth.

BEN. Where does such a beast really live?

WIL. Such a beast does not really live at all.

SIM. Then how can it be slain?

WIL. Have you no imagination?

SIM. I cannot picture this foolish beast at all, that comes forth on four legs which are two legs, to be slain when it is not really alive.

WIL. Such things live in the world of imagination.

BEN. Where in the world is that?

WIL. Why, everywhere in the world. For no one could imagine the world without imagination.

This song is usually   SONG.
     omitted   WILKINS.

Perhaps you don't imagine how important nowadays
Is the part (outside a theatre) imagination plays;
For our life is like a playhouse, where the livers wouldn't act,
If our facts were never fancy, and our fancies always fact!
From the Laureate, who fancies that in any grassy prose
(Which is turned out in a metre) a poetic fancy glows,
To the Youth of one-and-twenty, who imagines when he dines
That he doesn't fancy any but the most expensive wines!

He will take a glass of sherry,
  And imagine it is nice
(Though it's only elderberry),
  If he pay a fancy price.
(But the elderberry, nowadays, is going out of use,
And the younger current fancy is the berry of the goose!)

There's the Boy who fancies smoking is a pleasure so profound
That he'll very soon imagine that it makes the world go
    round;
And the Law-Case, where you fancy there is money to be got,
But the Law is such a lottery—and Lawyers draw the lot!
The imaginary Invalid, who fancies she is ill,
After reading the advertisement of some one's patent pill,
Will hurry to her doctor, whom she counts a " perfect dear "
(For his practice makes him perfect, and I don't know what
    a year).
  For the doctor is in luck, and
    Heavy fees will never lack,
  Whom the ladies call " a duck " (and
    Other doctors call a quack).
And the honour of the medical profession, as you'll see,
With imaginative patients is a matter of degree!
To those about to marry, don't imagine you are doves
Who can bill and coo for ever and be happy with your loves.
Imagine you can bill and coo for ever if you will,
But don't imagine turtle doves can coo without a bill;
Don't imagine that a cottage loaf is ever fancy bread,
And don't imagine everything is butter that is spread;
Don't imagine, if your grocer is particularly bland,
That you need not take your sugar with a grain or two of
    sand!

  And if the kitchen boiler
    Should induce you to employ
  That contemplative toiler,
    A plumber with his boy,
When at last he takes his coat off, don't imagine he will
    plumb—
That's the moment *he'll* imagine that his dinner hour has
    come!   [*Exit with* SIMKINS *and* BEN.

Enter JILL *with* TOM. *She gives him the deer-skin. Enter
  the Pages.*

JILL.   You'll do this?

TOM.   For thy sake.   [*Exit.*

FIRST PAGE. Come here, girl! I understand not this plot of
Essex very clearly.

JILL. Why, tis clearer than the Queen's conscience—which it is planned to clear. It is to prevent her vengeance pursuing Bessie Throckmorton, so that Bessie may marry Raleigh. So Raleigh will be out of the way of Essex in the Queen's favour when he is married, which some call marred.

SECOND PAGE. Well?

JILL. Well, to this end, and for the purpose of startling the Queen, the big Forester will appear to her anon in the guise of Herne the Hunter, and all of you here will pretend you see him not. So the Queen will think he appears to her alone, for a warning—if you tell your falsehoods fearlessly. Essex has arranged it with the common folk.

FIRST PAGE. The jest likes me well!

SECOND PAGE. Oddsfish! I like it not. I like not the thought of frightening a woman, be she Queen or common.

FIRST PAGE. Thou art frightened thyself!

SECOND PAGE. Nay. But it lies against my conscience to lie against my conscience, and I'll not lie to the Queen, who is my conscience. I'll have none of it.

PAGE. Then go—and pay thy taxes!

Enter ESSEX *and* ELIZABETH.

ESSEX. I pray you rest here, madam, a little, by Herne's Oak.

ELIZA. 'Twill soon be dusk.

ESSEX. Yes, madam. But there is nothing to fear from Herne. He only appears, they say, when the Sovereign contemplates—

ELIZA. What?

ESSEX. A crime, madam!

ELIZA. Ah!

ESSEX. Which is the same as if they said not at all. For the Queen can do no wrong.

WIL. God save the Queen.

ELIZA. What's this?

Enter others.

ESSEX. 'Tis a Masque, madam, which they have prepared for your pleasure. I pray you listen to it—if—

ELIZA. It may distract me. We will listen to it—but see that it is short. I'll not stay here till the sun set. What character do you play, knave?

WIL. Apart from the Prologue, I play two characters, madam. First, the King of Egypt, whose daughter is to be sacrificed to the Dragon, and then St. George himself, who rescues the lady.

ESSEX. Proceed with the action of the play.

(Those impersonating the Seven Champions commence to sing)
" We are Seven Champions of Christendom."

ESSEX *(stopping them.)* Omit the Prologue.

(WILKINS puts up a sign on which is written "This is a Palace.")

WIL.   I am the King of Egypt—yet I frown!
My heart, once light as a feather, now is down!

ESSEX. Stay! The Queen cares not for the humour which is mere juggling with words, such as " My heart, once light as a feather, now is down." There is a play on the words "down" and " feather," and if a play hang only on a play of words, the play may go hang for a play of words only. See to it!

WIL. Sir, I am no servile imitator of Shakespeare, but he hath his good points, and he hath sometimes made a point with a play of words.

ELIZA. Shakespeare is a writer—*I* am a critic!

WIL. God save the Queen!

ESSEX. Proceed with the action.

(WILKINS changes scene to " Another Part of the Palace.")

WIL. Enter several female attendants, singing and dancing.

ELIZA. Why are the attendants dancing?

WIL. Because, madam, they are dancing attendance—on the King.

Enter Dancing Girls.

(WILKINS changes scene to " A Garden with Fountains.")

WIL.   O happy maids, why do ye dance and sing?

MAR.   Because it is our nature to, O King!

WIL.   Nature! I gaze around, and it appears
All nature smiles, while I alone shed tears!
O cruel Nature, mother of us all,
Yet of all mothers most unnatural!
To-day at dawn the joyful sun did rise—

ELIZA. 'Tis the way of the world—and it will soon set!

ESSEX. Of your good nature leave the ill-nature of nature, and proceed with the action. The Queen is impatient.

WIL. *(after changing scene to " A Rocky Desert ".)*
Ye do not know what duty brings me here?
It is to sacrifice my daughter dear
Unto the Dragon, which, 'tis understood,
Lies lurking near us! She must be his food.

MAR.   Why must you sacrifice our fair Princess
Unto the Dragon?

WIL.   Shall I tell you?

MAR.   Yes!

ELIZA. No! It is enough that the Princess consents to be sacrificed. Doubtless she has good reason.

WIL. Her reason hath left her, for dread of the Dragon.

ESSEX. Well, well, let her enter without her reason, so she enters quickly.

WIL. " Enter the Princess Sabra with no reason. Music."

The PRINCESS enters, impersonated by the May Queen.

PRINCESS.   Oh, father, father, father, father—dost
             Thou say that I must die to-day?

WIL.   I dust—

ESSEX. Nay, " I do! " " I do! " Though you be King of Egypt, yet speak the Queen's English.

WIL. " Dust " is the right word, my lord.

ELIZA. Argue not, but say " I do! "

PRIN.   Oh, father, father, father, father—dost
             Thou say that I must die to-day?

WIL.   I do
             My head, and answer—

ESSEX. What is it you do to your head?

WIL. I put dust upon it, sir—as a sign of sorrow. 'Tis an Oriental custom.

ELIZA. Then suit the action to the words, and the words to the action.

PRIN.   Oh, father, father, father, father—dost
             Thou say that I must die to-day?

WIL.   I dust
             My head, and answer, " Yes, my child, thou must! "

DUET.

WILKINS *and* PRINCESS.

PRIN.   Oh, here's a to-do to die to-day
             At a minute or two to two,
             A thing distinctly hard to say,
             But a harder thing to do.

> For they'll beat a tattoo at two to two,
> A rat-a-tattoo at two—Boohoo!
> And the Dragon will come
> When it hears the drum
> At a minute or two to two to-day,
> At a minute or two to two!

WIL.   Why hullabaloo? You die to-day
> At a minute or two to two,
> A thing distinctly hard to say
> But an easy thing to do!
>   For they'll beat a tattoo at two to two,
>   A rat-a-tat-tat tattoo—for you!
> And the Dragon will come
> When he hears the drum;
> There's nothing for *you* to do but stay,
> And the Dragon will do for you!

ELIZA.   Stop! Enough! (*To* ESSEX.) Do you hear that?
                       (*A hunting horn is heard.*)

ESSEX.   I hear nothing.

ELIZA.   A hunting horn—faint and ghostly! Look!

(*She points to back, where* TOM *rises from the bracken, dressed as Herne the Hunter, against the red of the sunset.*)

ESSEX.   I see nothing! (*To others.*) Do you?

BEN.   No!

SIMKINS.   Nor I!

WIL.   Nor I! (*Giving broad wink at* ESSEX.) But if it were Herne the Hunter himself—

ELIZA.   Peace, I say! (*To* ESSEX.) You see nothing—there?

ESSEX.   Nothing but a gnarled tree against the sun.

ELIZA.   Then the sun has blinded me. I see red—all red. Give me your hand, Essex.

ESSEX.   With all my heart. (*Aside.*) 'Tis what we played for.

(*As* ESSEX *is leading off* ELIZABETH *the Fool, disguised as Apothecary, enters and approaches.*)

FOOL.   The drug, madam!

ELIZA.   I have changed my mind.

(*Alarm bell heard in distance. A Messenger enters breathlessly.*)

MES. The prisoners have escaped, madam—Mistress Throck-morton and the witch girl.

ELIZA. Let them go! They are—pardoned!

JILL. God save the Queen!

ELIZA. Ah!

MAY Q. The witch!

(JILL *runs off*.)

ALL. The witch! She's a witch!

ESSEX. The Queen has pronounced her innocent. She is pardoned once for all, like the other. Who'll go back on the Queen's word? [*Exit with* ELIZABETH.

(JILL *brings on* BESSIE *and* RALEIGH.)

JILL. Come—you are safe.

BESS. Safe?

RAL. They are ringing the alarm.

BESS. 'Tis our death bell!

WIL. Nay, nay—your wedding bell. The Queen has pardoned you, as I planned—as *I* planned! Take your Maid Marion, sir, and we'll play a Robin Hood's Wedding, in which I'll play King Richard the Lionheart. What say you?

RAL. With all my heart!

ALL. Aye! A Robin Hood's Wedding!

FINALE.

RAL.
    Who'll come, said Robin Hood,
      Who'll come to my wedding?

JILL.
      All those who love
      The blue sky above,
    And the green grass to lie upon—
      'Tis better than bedding!

ALL.
    All such are welcome
      At Robin Hood's wedding.

RAL.
    Who'll tie the lovers' knot
      At Robin Hood's wedding?

SIM
      I, said the Friar,
      And I'll lead the choir,
    Quoth Friar Tuck to Robin Hood,
      At Robin Hood's wedding.

RAL.
    Who'll be the groom, his man,
      At Robin Hood's wedding?

TOM	I, said Big John, My Lincoln I'll don, Quoth Little John to Robin Hood, At Robin Hood's wedding.
RAL.	Who'll give the bride away At Robin Hood's wedding?
WIL.	I, said the King, My Queen too I bring, Quoth Richard unto Robin Hood, At Robin Hood's wedding.
RAL.	Who'll dance with Robin Hood At Robin Hood's wedding?
BESSIE.	I, said his bride, I'll dance by thy side, Quoth Marion to Robin Hood, At Robin Hood's wedding.
ALL.	Then God save the King! And God save the Queen! And let us all sing And dance on the green In memory of Robin Hood, In memory of Marion, And all the merry men and maids Who danced at their wedding.

With a hey, jolly Robin, &c.

(*A dance.* QUEEN ELIZABETH *and* ESSEX *enter on high
ground at back, led on by the Fool. He points out to
the* QUEEN *the group of "Robin Hood's Wedding,"
similar to that formed by the Morris Dancers in Act I., in
which* RALEIGH *and* BESSIE *are now the central figures.*)

CURTAIN.

Lightning Source UK Ltd.
Milton Keynes UK
UKHW021010200820
368550UK00009B/1255